CW01512562

Original title:
Faint Shards Along the Elf Cull

Author: Paulina Pähkel
ISBN HARDBACK: 978-1-80562-910-8
ISBN PAPERBACK: 978-1-80564-431-6

Shimmers of Unraveled Mysteries

In shadows deep where secrets dwell,
The moonlight casts its gentle spell.
With every shimmer, tales unfold,
Of ancient maps and heroes bold.

A flicker bright, a glint of gold,
In whispered winds, the truth retold.
Through faded paths, where echoes roam,
The heart finds solace, the mind finds home.

Each mystery a thread, a woven dance,
To seek the unknown, to take a chance.
Beneath the stars, with bated breath,
We chase the shadows, defy our death.

With gentle hands, the story we weave,
In every dusk, a promise to believe.
For every turn of fate's grand wheel,
There lie the dreams our hearts conceal.

So follow now, the spark that glows,
Through tangled woods, where magic flows.
For in the dark, our spirits soar,
Unraveled mysteries forevermore.

The Light Behind the Whispering Leaves

Amidst the grove where sunlight beams,
The leaves confide in whispered dreams.
They sway and dance in playful flight,
Unveiling secrets in dappled light.

Each rustle speaks of stories past,
Of fleeting moments, shadows cast.
In twilight's glow, the magic thrives,
With every breath, the woodland lives.

The heart of nature, pure and true,
In gentle shades of varied hue.
A bumping brook, a tale it weaves,
As sunbeams flicker on whispered leaves.

So linger here, let worries cease,
Embrace the soft and tranquil peace.
For in this realm, we find our grace,
In every rustling leaf's embrace.

And as the stars begin to gleam,
We dance to nature's eve-lit dream.
With every spirit, every sigh,
The leaves will whisper as we fly.

Mystical Currents of Forgotten Lore

In shadows deep, the whispers creep,
Secrets of old, the ancients keep.
Forgotten paths where starlight gleams,
Flowing like water, the world's lost dreams.

Beneath the moon, the rivers sigh,
Carrying tales of the days gone by.
With each ripple, the stories unfold,
A tapestry woven from threads of gold.

Through misty woods where silence reigns,
Echoes of magic in temporal chains.
Every leaf tells a tale of yore,
For those who listen, and seek to explore.

In twilight's grasp, the spirits dance,
Entwined in an everlasting trance.
Their laughter rings, a silvery bell,
Inviting hearts to break the spell.

So journey forth, brave soul, and seek,
The currents that call, the tides that speak.
For within the lore, a light you find,
A treasure of wisdom for heart and mind.

Illumination Through the Veil of Time

When dawn's first light begins to show,
The past ignites, a golden glow.
Through veils of time, the shadows blend,
A glimpse of what the fates intend.

Each moment holds a myriad of dreams,
Woven together in silken seams.
The ages whisper, a soft refrain,
In echoes of joy, and hints of pain.

With every tick of the clock's embrace,
The dance of memory begins to trace.
A flicker of hope in stories untold,
An ember of warmth in the chilling cold.

In twilight's haze, we seek the spark,
A flickering flame in the gathering dark.
The threads of life in colors bright,
Illuminating paths in the depth of night.

So heed the moments that shimmer and shine,
For through the veil flows the design.
Each heartbeat draws us to intertwine,
In the luminous dance of the grand divine.

Shards of Memory in the Sylvan Silence

Amidst the trees where shadows dwell,
The forest breathes a secret spell.
In every rustle, a story weaves,
Shards of memory, the heart retrieves.

The whispers of leaves in gentle tones,
Echo the laughter of ancient stones.
Paths of enchantment laid with care,
Call to the wanderers, lost in despair.

Through sylvan sanctuaries, silence roams,
Cradling the thoughts of long-lost homes.
In stillness, wisdom awaits to find,
A refuge for the restless mind.

With every step on the mossy floor,
The echoes of ages resound evermore.
Each shard a moment, a piece of soul,
Gathered together, they make us whole.

Under the canopy where shadows play,
The heart of the forest will guide the way.
To discover the truth in the gentle embrace,
Of memory's shards in this timeless space.

Harmonics of the Ageless Wood

In the heart of the wood where secrets sing,
A symphony of nature begins to spring.
Each bird's call a note, so clear and bright,
Painting the air with pure delight.

Gentle breezes, a soft caress,
Whispers of the leaves in their sweet dress.
A melody crafted by time and space,
Echoing softly in nature's grace.

Luminous streams through sunlight thread,
Dance to the rhythm where the ancients tread.
In the cadence of life, we find our part,
The harmonics weaving through the heart.

With every footfall upon the ground,
The ageless wood sings, profound and sound.
An orchestra of life, infinite, vast,
Bridging the future, the present, the past.

So close your eyes and just listen well,
To the stories and songs, they have to tell.
For in the woods, with its mystic air,
The harmonics of life are always there.

Intrigues of the Starlit Canopy

Under the moon's soft embrace,
Whispers of secrets take flight.
Stars weave tales of old,
In the tapestry of night.

Among the trees, shadows dance,
Each flicker tells a story.
Beneath the canopy's glance,
Echoes of forgotten glory.

A breeze carries ghostly sighs,
As leaves rustle in reply.
The world below holds its breath,
While mysteries linger nearby.

In this realm, time stands still,
The heartbeats sync with the sky.
Dreams intermingle with starlight,
Guided by a gentle sigh.

With every glance to the heavens,
Hope blooms in the silent air.
Such wonders hidden in shadows,
Unraveled for those who dare.

A Tapestry of Dreams and Sorrows

Threads of joy and sorrow blend,
In the woven fabric of fate.
Each stitch a realm to transcend,
Crafting tales delicate and great.

Each dream a flickering spark,
Intertwined with the past's embrace.
Underneath the night so dark,
Memories dance in their place.

The loom of life, ever turning,
With choices that shape our design.
Burning embers, forever yearning,
In the tapestry, we align.

Soft echoes of laughter and tears,
Tell stories of brave hearts and fears.
In each moment, we find our way,
As the night melds into day.

A tale of strength, a whisper of grace,
A journey marked by the chase.
With resilience, we thread our seams,
In a tapestry of hopes and dreams.

Beneath the Canopy of Silenced Dreams

Beneath a veil of twilight's mist,
Where shadows gather and sigh.
A hush falls over the forest,
As forgotten wishes slip by.

Whispers of hope, barely heard,
Drift on the breath of the trees.
In stillness, the heart's voice stirred,
Longing for moments like these.

The stars above twinkle dimly,
As secrets weave through the air.
Lost in a dream's silent hymn,
Rests the tale of the unaware.

Each leaf a keeper of stories,
Of laughter, love, and despair.
In the quiet enveloping glories,
Echoes of souls linger there.

In this sanctuary of shadows,
Where dreams await the dawn's light,
They pulse in the heart's quiet throes,
Beneath the canopy's silent night.

Dreams Intertwined with Breaths of Nature

In the cradle of the forest deep,
Dreams entwine with nature's breath.
Whispers echo as shadows creep,
Holding the secrets of life and death.

Amidst the rustling leaves of green,
A melody softly plays.
Dancing on breezes unseen,
Guiding hearts through the maze.

Moonlight spills on the earth,
And sparkles like fairy dust.
Each moment of magic a birth,
In dreams that linger, we trust.

The stream hums a tranquil tune,
Connecting the world's distant shores.
A symphony beneath the moon,
As nature whispers and roars.

Within this enchanted embrace,
We find our spirits set free.
In the dance of time and space,
Dreams and nature's harmony.

Ghostly Emotions in Whispering Pines

In the hush of twilight's call,
Whispers echo through the tall.
Ghostly shadows weave and play,
In the pines, they dance away.

Between the branches, secrets sigh,
Memories linger, never die.
A heart once lost, now faintly glows,
In the dark, where silence grows.

The breeze carries tales of yore,
Sighs of those who roamed before.
Flickering lights in the night's embrace,
Illuminate a forgotten place.

Restless spirits, longing still,
Seeking warmth, a moment's thrill.
In the trees, their voices blend,
A haunting song that will not end.

Beneath the veil of stars above,
Whispering pines call out with love.
Emotions dance like fleeting air,
In ghostly realms, they bare their care.

The Dance of Sighing Ferns

In the glade where shadows twirl,
Eager ferns begin to swirl.
Softly sighing with the breeze,
They unveil their timeless tease.

Each frond a story yet unknown,
In nature's depths, their secrets sewn.
They bend and sway, a graceful flight,
In moonlit dreams of gentle night.

Their whispers brush against the ground,
In harmony, a rhythm found.
A dance that echoes through the air,
With every sigh, a world laid bare.

Beneath the stars, they find their tune,
In concert with the silver moon.
A symphony of soft delight,
In the heart of the quiet night.

The dance of ferns, a fleeting spark,
Exploring silence, deep and dark.
They teach us all to sway and bend,
In gentle rhythms that never end.

Secrets Hidden 'Neath the Old Tree

Beneath the roots, where shadows dwell,
Lie whispered tales that time won't tell.
Each gnarled limb, a storyteller,
Guarding secrets, soft and stellar.

Rays of sun and drops of rain,
Nurturing dreams that bear the pain.
Shared by creatures who take their rest,
In the heart of the tree, they're blessed.

The wise old bark, a shield of ages,
Holding truths like weathered pages.
If one should pause, and listen well,
They'll hear the mysteries that swell.

In the rustle of the leaves above,
Lies a language rooted in love.
The wind carries a soft decree,
Of all the wonders the tree can see.

So crouch around and drink it in,
Feel the magic that dwells within.
For beneath this ancient remedy,
Lie the secrets hidden 'neath the old tree.

Ethereal Glimmers at Dusk's Door

As the sun begins to fade,
Colors shift in soft parade.
Glimmers dance on twilight's skin,
Welcoming night, where dreams begin.

The horizon blushes, a gentle sigh,
As day bids farewell, with a lonesome cry.
Stars awaken with a shimmering grace,
Casting whispers across the space.

In the hush of fading light,
Ethereal sparkles take their flight.
They trail like wishes, woven and spun,
Beneath the gathering of the moon's fun.

With each tick of the clock's soft chime,
Moments slow, as if to rhyme.
A tapestry of night unfolds,
With stories woven in shades of gold.

So linger long at dusk's wide door,
For in the shadows, there's so much more.
Ethereal glimmers beckon you near,
To dance with dreams, without a fear.

Flickers of Time in Forgotten Glades

In whispered woods where shadows play,
The flickers of time dance and sway.
Each leaf a tale of days gone by,
Beneath the arching, endless sky.

Glimmers of light through branches weave,
Secrets of dreams in which we believe.
Echoes of laughter beneath the boughs,
Nature's reverence, a sacred vow.

A shimmering brook sings soft and low,
Inviting the heart to wander slow.
With every step, a memory's kiss,
In this glade, there's a fleeting bliss.

Time lingers here, a gentle pause,
Reminding us of the world's cause.
In every flicker, a moment preserved,
In each breath of life, we're truly served.

Through forgotten glades, so rich and rare,
We find our souls, laid gently bare.
As time dissolves in twilight's hue,
We grasp the magic, forever new.

The Gentle Touch of Abandoned Echoes

In quiet halls where whispers dwell,
The echoes tell a timeless spell.
Faint laughter lingers in the air,
A gentle touch, a distant care.

The dust of ages settles slow,
On memories that ebb and flow.
Each corner holds a ghostly trace,
Of lives once lived in this still place.

Sunlight filters through the leaves,
Casting shadows that time retrieves.
In every creak, in every sigh,
Resides a story waiting nearby.

Walls that once knew vibrant cheer,
Now cradle silence, yearning near.
Yet in the stillness, hope remains,
For whispers dance in autumn rains.

Upon each step, nostalgia spills,
Stirring the heart with gentle thrills.
These echoes softly, sweetly blend,
In memories, the soul we mend.

Twilight's Soft Embrace of Memory

As twilight wraps the world in gold,
The whispers of memory, soft and bold.
Each star above a wish anew,
In gentle dusk, our dreams accrue.

With fading light, the shadows grow,
A tender touch, a soothing glow.
The evening calls with threads of grace,
As time paints memories in this space.

Each moment's hue, a fleeting glance,
In twilight's arms, we softly dance.
With every breath, the heart takes flight,
In shadows deep, we find our light.

The sky, a canvas, ever changing,
Our stories linger, rearranging.
In twilight's hush, the past entwines,
A tapestry where love defines.

So let the night enfold us tight,
As memories gleam in soft moonlight.
In twilight's care, we come alive,
Together in these dreams, we thrive.

Where the Lost Spirits Gently Weep

In misty veils where shadows creep,
The lost spirits linger, softly weep.
Their sighs like breath from autumn's chill,
Echo through valleys, vast and still.

Beneath the stars, their stories glow,
Whispers of love in winds that blow.
In every tear, a journey fades,
As they seek solace in twilight glades.

The nightingale serenades the heart,
Giving voice to each lost part.
In dreams, they walk through memories dear,
Embracing all they can't hold near.

Yet in their sorrow, beauty lies,
In melancholy's soft goodbyes.
With every sigh, the world remembers,
The warmth of souls through darkened embers.

So let them weep, their tales unfold,
In silvered whispers, secrets told.
For in this space, where memories weep,
The lost find peace, their dreams to keep.

Enchanted Reflections in Dusk

In the twilight where shadows play,
The whispers weave a soft ballet.
Stars awaken, blinking bright,
Guiding dreams on gentle flight.

Mirrored pools like glassy eyes,
Hold the secrets of the skies.
A silver beam, a fleeting glance,
Invite the night to join the dance.

Dancing lights in fading gleam,
Call the heart to chase a dream.
With every sigh, the night does bloom,
In magical, enchanting gloom.

Softly now, the world unwinds,
Where the dusky magic binds.
In every rustle, every sound,
A quiet charm is still to be found.

As moonlight stitches night and day,
We'll drift where glowing fairies play.
Forever held in twilight's thrall,
In enchanted dusk, we find it all.

Silhouettes of the Forest's Heart

Beneath the boughs, the shadows creep,
Where ancient secrets lie so deep.
Silhouettes of trees entwined,
Guard the wisdom left behind.

Rustling leaves sing sweet and low,
In the forest's heart, the echoes flow.
Every branch, a tale to tell,
Of creatures hidden under spell.

Paths are twisted, winding true,
Leading souls to wander through.
Emerald canopies above,
Embrace the hush, the song of love.

Moonlit clearings softly gleam,
Where the night is but a dream.
In shadows deep, we're not alone,
The forest's heart is a gentle home.

With every step, we roam and find,
The magic sewn into the mind.
Here among the ancient trees,
Our spirits dance upon the breeze.

Celestial Whispers among Willows

Beneath the willows, whispers sway,
In silvered light, they dance and play.
Celestial secrets softly shared,
In the tranquil air, we're bared.

Each drooping branch, a gentle sigh,
As stars spill forth from velvet sky.
The moon's embrace, a tender glow,
Guiding hearts where breezes blow.

Rippling waters, echoes near,
Reflecting dreams that linger here.
Among the roots, life flows anew,
Where love and hope are born and grew.

Listen close, the night does hum,
With tales of ages yet to come.
In whispered winds, our hopes ascend,
As willows sway, they mend and blend.

In this embrace, we find our grace,
With nature's rhythm, we find our place.
Celestial whispers light our way,
Guiding souls till break of day.

Secrets Bound in Moss and Mist

In the glen where shadows wane,
Mossy secrets softly reign.
Wrapped in mist, the world stands still,
Holding magic, finding will.

Beneath the cover, life will stir,
Softly hidden, yet astir.
Each dewdrop holds a whispered fate,
In silent corners, love awaits.

Winding paths of emerald hue,
Lead us deeper, thoughts renew.
As ferns unfurl with gentle grace,
In the hidden, we find our space.

Echoes linger, soft and light,
Secrets shared through the night.
In every shadow, every twist,
Lies the beauty none can resist.

The morning sun begins to break,
Revealing treasures nature makes.
In moss and mist, we come to see,
The heart of magic, wild and free.

Shrouded Gaze of the Ancient Sylph

In twilight's breath, where shadows dwell,
A sylph whispers secrets of the well.
Her gaze, a shroud of mist and light,
Holds ages lost to the coming night.

Among the trees, her laughter sings,
A memory wrapped in delicate wings.
With every sigh, the zephyrs weave,
Tales of magic that few believe.

Her presence drifts like autumn leaves,
In the silence, where the moon deceives.
She dances softly on the breeze,
Eldritch tales carried through the trees.

Yet, gaze not too long, for time will bend,
And ancient truths may twist, transcend.
In her embrace, the lost may find,
The thin veil drawn 'twixt fate and mind.

A whisper lingers, soft and rare,
Of sylphs that tread in enchanted air.
Should you seek her, take heed and pause,
For in her gaze lies the world's lost cause.

Memories etched in Moonlit Tides

Beneath the sky where starlight spills,
The ocean whispers with hidden thrills.
Each wave a tale from ages past,
A fleeting moment, forever cast.

Moonlit paths on silver sea,
Cradle dreams of what could be.
Rippling echoes of laughter sweet,
In each soft swell, the heart's retreat.

As tides embrace the mystical shore,
Old memories rise, forevermore.
With every ebb, a story flows,
Of loves once known, the heart's true throes.

Gaze upon the watery glass,
Where time's reflection will always pass.
In the moon's glow, secrets entwine,
The sea recalls what it once called mine.

So cherish nights when stars align,
For every wave, a forgotten sign.
In the depths of night's soft glides,
Our souls are etched in moonlit tides.

Faded Murmurs of Elven Lore

In the glade where shadows play,
Elven whispers drift away.
Legends linger in the breeze,
As time ebbs past the ancient trees.

Stories woven with gossamer thread,
Of lost empires and words unsaid.
Each murmur carries a timeless grace,
With echoes that time cannot erase.

The sunlight filters through the leaves,
Where elven kind in twilight grieves.
A lore of magic, soft and pure,
In the silence, their hearts endure.

Faded memories entwine with dreams,
In moonlit glades, where starlight gleams.
With every sigh, a world appears,
As ancient lore dissolves in tears.

Here, among the roots and stone,
The secrets of ages linger alone.
So heed the whispers, soft, forlorn,
For in them, the elven heart is born.

Fissures through which Dreams Drift

In the fabric of night, a rift unfurls,
Where dreams take flight in spiraled swirls.
Each fissure hums with ancient grace,
A portal to find our hidden place.

Through twilight's veil, the echoes glide,
In wisps and shadows, we confide.
Thoughts like wisps of smoke unfurl,
To dance in secrets, a shadowed whirl.

In this realm where wishes weave,
What we lose, yet still believe.
A tapestry spun from hopes untold,
In every dream, a glimpse of gold.

Gaze through the cracks, seek what's beneath,
Where visions bloom in wild wreath.
Through the fissures, our souls shall drift,
In the warm embrace of destiny's gift.

So take my hand and close your eyes,
Together we'll chase the evening skies.
For in the night, our spirits lift,
Through fissures of dreams, we find our gift.

Whispers of Forgotten Magic

In the heart of the old wood,
Where shadows breathe and fade,
The whispers of ages call out,
With secrets that time betrayed.

Wandering spirits flutter,
In glimmers of starlit air,
Each flickering light a promise,
Of magic lost everywhere.

Ancient stones hum with wisdom,
Their voices a soft, gentle breeze,
Songs of the past resonate,
In rustling leaves and the trees.

A glint of a wand forgotten,
Lies deep in the emerald moss,
Tales of enchantment and wonder,
In every sigh, every gloss.

So linger a moment longer,
Feel the pulse of the night,
For whispers of forgotten magic,
Still dance in the silver light.

Echoes in the Moonlit Grove

In the stillness of twilight,
Underneath a shimmering sky,
Moonbeams twist through the branches,
As shadows play and sigh.

The air is thick with stories,
Of creatures both fierce and kind,
Echoes linger in the silence,
Of adventures left behind.

A fox darts through the thickets,
With eyes like glowing stones,
Chasing the dreams of the forest,
Where magic feels at home.

The murmurs of ancient oak trees,
Breathe life into the night,
While silver streams weave secrets,
In soft, silken moonlight.

So wander through the grove, dear heart,
Let the echoes guide your way,
For magic pulses in the shadows,
In the moonlit dance of day.

Fragments of Enchanted Echoes

Fragments of dreams flutter softly,
Like leaves caught in the breeze,
Each shimmer a tale forgotten,
Whispered 'neath the trees.

Listen close to the silence,
It speaks in riddles and rhymes,
Of worlds beyond our vision,
And hearts lost in the times.

The laughter of sprites fills the air,
With echoes of joy and tears,
A tapestry woven of starlight,
Softening all our fears.

Each fragment a spell of magic,
A puzzle yet to be known,
In the hush of the evening's glow,
Enchantment begs to be shown.

So gather these pieces tightly,
Let your spirit take flight,
For fragments of enchanted echoes,
Transform in the fading light.

Shadows of Lost Realms

In shadows of forgotten kingdoms,
Where echoes once held sway,
Silent whispers of lost realms,
Begin to drift away.

The castle walls now crumble,
With ivy winding tight,
Each stone a keeper of secrets,
In the heart of the night.

Faded banners of glory,
Sway softly in the chill,
Drawing dreams from the ether,
As time begins to still.

The spirits weave through the twilight,
Their stories traced in mist,
Guardians of forgotten lore,
In shadows' gentle tryst.

So dare to seek these lost realms,
In the half-light's soft embrace,
For shadows of ancient magic,
Hold beauty in their grace.

Songs of Silvered Leaves in Time's Recess

In whispers soft, the leaves do sigh,
They tell of tales that drift on high.
Beneath the boughs where shadows weave,
Awake the dreams we once believed.

Each silvered leaf a story spun,
Of battles lost and victories won.
In twilight's glow, a dance begins,
With laughter sweet, where sorrow thins.

The brook recalls what time forgot,
Its gentle song, a soothing thought.
With every ripple, time will trace,
The fleeting joys we long to chase.

So linger here where moments pause,
In nature's arms, we find our cause.
The silvered leaves in twilight's glow,
Hold every secret we must know.

As night descends, the stars will gleam,
A guardian of each whispered dream.
And in the heart, the song remains,
Of silvered leaves and soft refrains.

Phantoms in the Veil of Stillness

In quietude, the phantoms play,
Veiled in mist, they drift away.
A silence deep, where echoes cling,
And shadows dance with whispered spring.

They hold the tales of long ago,
In every breath, the memories flow.
A tapestry of light and dark,
Each thread a flicker, each thread a spark.

With every sigh, they softly speak,
Of hidden worlds and futures sleek.
In stillness' grasp, the moments freeze,
As time unravels, just to tease.

Through veils of night, a shimmer bright,
Guides wandering souls to find their light.
In phantoms' grace, we find our way,
Through the whispering woods where shadows play.

So heed the call, let silence reign,
For in the still, there's joy and pain.
Embrace the phantoms, hear their song,
In the calm of night, we all belong.

Reflections of a Timeless Echo

In mirrors deep, the past is found,
A timeless echo, soft and sound.
Each glance reflects a world anew,
With shadows bright in shades of blue.

The heart remembers, beats in tune,
With whispered dreams beneath the moon.
In echoes soft, the stories flow,
Of love and loss that come and go.

The river's song, a gentle guide,
Through life's twists, we must abide.
A ripple cast in time's embrace,
Each moment holds a sacred place.

Beneath the stars that light the night,
The echoes weave a tapestry bright.
In every heartbeat, every breath,
We find the dance of life and death.

So let us learn from what has been,
Discover secrets held within.
In timeless echoes, wisdom glows,
A path to where our spirit grows.

Enchanted Pathways of the Forgotten

In forests deep, where magic lies,
The pathways weave beneath the skies.
With each step taken, secrets bloom,
And whispers chase away the gloom.

The ancient trees hold stories warm,
Of love's embrace and weathered storm.
In every knot, in every grain,
The echo of a sweet refrain.

As twilight wraps the world in gold,
The enchanted paths begin to unfold.
With every turn, a new surprise,
A wonder hidden from our eyes.

Through tangled vines and dappled light,
We wander free, our hearts in flight.
In memories etched, the stories flare,
Of journeys taken, of love laid bare.

So heed the call of pathways grand,
Where dreams are woven, hand in hand.
In enchanted woods, we find our right,
A sanctuary of shared delight.

Ethereal Flickers of Forgotten Lore

In twilight's grasp, where whispers play,
The secrets of the night hold sway.
With stars like candles in the dark,
Each twinkling light, a hidden spark.

The ancient tomes, with dust adorned,
Speak tales of worlds, forever mourned.
With pages worn, their wisdom gleams,
A tapestry spun from lost dreams.

In shadows deep, the magic stirs,
Enchanting realms that time obscures.
With every heartbeat, an echo calls,
Through silent halls where memory falls.

Their fleeting forms, like mist, arise,
To dance beneath the winking skies.
A fleeting glimpse, a fleeting breath,
The lore of ages conquering death.

When night descends, and silence sings,
The world awakens to hidden things.
In ethereal flickers, truth reveals,
The tangled fate that time conceals.

Twists of Time in Evernight's Embrace

In evernight's soft, velvety fold,
Time dances lightly, stories unfold.
With every tick, a dream takes flight,
In shadows spun from the fabric of night.

Through ancient woods where echoes thrive,
The whispers of the past come alive.
They twist and turn, around every bend,
In a labyrinth where beginnings end.

The clock strikes twelve, and worlds collide,
With memories buried, where phantoms hide.
Beneath the stars, the ageless roam,
Seeking solace far from home.

Each heartbeat feels like a choice undone,
A fleeting chance, a race they run.
In tangled fates, so fragile and fine,
Eternity beckons with a siren's line.

In shadows deep, where hope wrestles dread,
Time unravels where the brave once tread.
And in that space, hearts intertwine,
Twists of fate in the grand design.

The Gossamer Path of Elven Memories

Through tangled woods where moonlight glows,
The gossamer path of legend flows.
With every step, a tale unfolds,
Of whispered dreams and secrets told.

Elven echoes soft as the breeze,
Carry songs from the ancient trees.
In every leaf, a heart's refrain,
Of love and loss, of joy and pain.

With nimble grace, they weave and sway,
In twilight's arms, where shadows play.
Their laughter mingles with the stars,
A dance of light, despite the scars.

Time bends softly on the glen,
Where memories linger now and then.
In every flicker, a fleeting glance,
A journey taken, a sacred dance.

Upon this path, where spirits dwell,
Beliefs entwined, in twilight's spell.
Through gossamer strands, their voices rise,
Elven memories, a timeless sigh.

Shadows Casting Longing Glances

In quiet corners, shadows dwell,
Casting glances like a fleeting spell.
They whisper secrets of love untold,
In the dusky light, their stories unfold.

With every flicker, a longing sigh,
As echoes of dreams in silence fly.
They stretch like fingers, reaching wide,
For moments lost where hopes abide.

Through velvet nights, their paths entwine,
With glimpses of sorrow, a bittersweet line.
In gentle curves, they softly weave,
A tapestry of hearts that grieve.

Beneath the stars, where wishes bloom,
Shadows cradle our deepest gloom.
In each embrace, a dance of fate,
A longing glance, forever wait.

So let them linger, these longing shades,
For in their depths, a love pervades.
Casting shadows where dreams are cast,
In the theater of the heart, they last.

The Forgotten Song of Leaf and Stone

In the quiet glen where shadows creep,
The whispers of the ancients sleep.
Leaves once danced in the breeze's sigh,
But now beneath the stillness lie.

Echoes linger of a song once bold,
Of tales of magic and treasures untold.
The stones remember, they softly hum,
As nature speaks, then falls quite numb.

The brook babbles in a language rare,
Carving stories in the crisp, cool air.
Moss clings gently to weathered roots,
Guarding secrets of forgotten pursuits.

A flicker of light weaves through the trees,
Revealing paths hidden by ancient weeds.
The songs of yore, they guide like stars,
Beneath the moon, they heal our scars.

So pause in this realm where dreams are spun,
For the song of the forest is never done.
Listen closely, let the heart attune,
To the sound of the earth, the sun, and the moon.

Echoes of Celestial Lament

In the midnight sky, where silence reigns,
Stars cry softly, their light like chains.
Each twinkle holds a ghostly tear,
Of wishes lost in the endless sphere.

The moon, a guardian of secrets old,
Watches over dreams that time has scrolled.
In its glow, forgotten voices sing,
A lament of hope, a sorrowful wing.

Galaxies spin in a tender waltz,
Each cosmic dance, a heart's vault.
Whirling memories of joys and fears,
In the vastness, they fade like years.

Comets streak across the night's embrace,
Leaving echoes of their fleeting grace.
Constellations weave a tapestry bright,
Reflecting love in the cloak of night.

So gaze aloft when the world feels grim,
Let the stars' lament become your hymn.
For in this canvas, we all belong,
A universe singing its timeless song.

Shards of Reflected Hope

In shards of glass, the light will dance,
Fractured hopes take a fleeting chance.
Reflected dreams in a rainbow bloom,
Filling the corners of a lonely room.

Each piece a wish, each crack a tale,
Where love and courage set the sail.
In brokenness, beauty finds its way,
Casting colors where shadows play.

Hope is fragile, yet fiercely bright,
Illuminating paths lost from sight.
Through the chaos, a promise remains,
That even in struggle, all love sustains.

So gather the shards, don't let them fall,
In this mosaic, we find our call.
United in fragments, we shape the dawn,
With each whispered hope, a new world drawn.

For every splinter holds a gleam,
A reminder of life's enduring dream.
Let us cherish the glow in misstep's keep,
For in every break, our spirits leap.

Tides of Memory in the Forest Depths

In the forest depths, where shadows weave,
Tides of memory ebb and leave.
Whispers of past in the rustling leaves,
Entwined with stories that the heart believes.

Streams flow gently, murmur serene,
Carrying echoes of what might have been.
Footsteps linger on dampened soil,
As time holds close the dreams we toil.

Moss blankets paths of wandering souls,
While ancient trees play their timeless roles.
Each breeze carries a tale to tell,
Of joy and sorrow, of rise and fell.

Beneath boughs heavy with memory's weight,
Lives a reminder of love and fate.
In every shadow, in every gleam,
The forest holds tight our shared dream.

So wander these pathways, embrace the flow,
For within the depths, our spirits grow.
The tides of memory, a sacred dance,
In the heart of nature, find our chance.

Reflections in the Glassy Lake

Beneath the willow's weeping boughs,
The lake lies still, a mirror bright.
It holds the secrets of the stars,
And whispers tales of silent night.

Each ripple casts a fleeting thought,
Of dreams that dance on silver beams.
It cradles hopes, both lost and sought,
In shimmering, quiet streams.

The moonlight dips, a gentle kiss,
Upon the surface, soft and clear.
It beckons forth a tranquil bliss,
To hearts that ache, to souls held dear.

Oh, glassy lake, you hold the past,
In every glance, a memory.
Through time's swift flow, your gaze holds fast,
As we unravel history.

With every breath, we share your peace,
In quiet moments, hope reborn.
So may your whispers never cease,
In twilight's hush, when day is worn.

The Link Between Light and Shade

In dusk's embrace, the shadows grow,
Where secrets lurk and whispers hide.
The balance sways, a dance we know,
　Between the light and dark inside.

The sun dips low, a fiery heart,
　Flames flicker out, retreating slow.
Yet in this twilight, worlds won't part,
For in the shade, new wonders glow.

Soft radiance meets the night's cool breath,
　A harmony, both bold and shy.
Life thriving here, despite of death,
　In every corner, dreams can fly.

The quiet hum of evening calls,
　An echo of the day once bright.
In shadows deep, a magic sprawls,
The link that binds both light and night.

With every dawn, the dance renews,
　A cycle spun, a tapestry.
In light and shade, we find our muse,
　The beauty in duality.

Flickering Hues of Beneath the Bough

Under branches thick with age,
The flickering hues of twilight play.
A canvas stretched, a living stage,
Where dreams and memories gently sway.

The whispers tease the evening air,
As fireflies weave their glowing lines.
Each spark a thought, a fleeting prayer,
In dusky realms where magic shines.

The soft embrace of night unfolds,
A cloak of velvet, rich and deep.
Within its depths, a story told,
Of secrets scattered, promises to keep.

Each color blends with shadows' grace,
In nature's brush, a brush of fate.
The moon appears, a gentle face,
To guard the dreams that stir and wait.

With every rustle, hearts take flight,
In flickering hues that softly glow.
Beneath the bough, the world feels right,
As magic dances, ever slow.

Chained Whispers in the Sylvan Night

In forests deep, where shadows scheme,
Chained whispers weave through mossy veil.
The ancient trees, with roots that dream,
Guard silent tales in twilight's pale.

Each rustling leaf a secret speaks,
Of world unseen, of realms entwined.
In echoes soft, the nighttime seeks,
A harmony that love has twined.

With starlit eyes, the owls converse,
As night unveils its hidden lore.
In sylvan paths, the heart's soft verse,
Plays on, forever more and more.

The moon shines through, a watchful guide,
As shadows twist and branch like fate.
In every sigh, the woods confide,
Their stories old, their whispers wait.

Oh, chained whispers in the night,
In eerie silence, we can roam.
Through sylvan dreams, we find our light,
In nature's arms, we find our home.

Celestial Threads of Twilight

In the dusk where shadows weave,
Stars begin their soft reprieve.
Whispers float on night's cool breath,
In silence, secrets dance with death.

Glistening orbs in skies so wide,
Call forth dreams that dare to glide.
Moonlit paths where wishes tread,
Awake the slumbering dreams long fed.

Threads of gold to stitch the night,
Woven tales of pure delight.
Elven laughter fills the space,
As twilight bathes the world in grace.

Glimmering hues where shadows play,
Heralding the end of day.
Each star a story yet untold,
In twilight's charm, the heart feels bold.

Through the vale of midnight's song,
A tapestry of night so strong.
Bathed in light from realms above,
We find the magic born of love.

Enigma of the Glimmering Glade

In a glade where whispers dwell,
Mysteries weave their secret spell.
Shimmering leaves in starlit beams,
Spin the fabric of our dreams.

Beneath the boughs of ancient trees,
Gentle breezes speak with ease.
Elders guard the tales of yore,
Inviting hearts to learn once more.

Silvery streams that softly flow,
Carry stories long ago.
In the dance of fireflies bright,
Magic twirls in pure delight.

Echoes linger, soft and clear,
In every breath, the truth draws near.
With every step, the world unfolds,
A tapestry of wonders bold.

So wander deep where shadows wait,
Unlock the doors that fate has strait.
For every glimmer hides a tale,
In this enchanting, timeless vale.

Specters of the Ethereal Vale

Where mist and memories entwine,
Linger the specters, soft divine.
Glimmering forms from shadows deep,
Awakening dreams from gentle sleep.

In the vale where silence reigns,
Echoes whisper of love's chains.
With graceful steps, they glide and sway,
In twilight's folds, they dance and play.

Winds carry tales of times gone by,
Through the heavens, spirits fly.
Veils of starlight lace the ground,
In ethereal realms, they're found.

Calling forth the heart's deep yearn,
From shadows, light begins to burn.
In the darkness, hope takes flight,
In the vale where day meets night.

With each breath, the night ignites,
Living dreams in endless sights.
Specters weave their timeless art,
In every soul, they leave a part.

Luminous Trails of Elven Dreams

Across the glen where starlight glows,
Luminous trails of magic flows.
Elven laughter fills the air,
As time surrenders to their care.

Glistening paths of silver light,
Guide the hearts through endless night.
In the whispering leaves' embrace,
Dreams awaken, bright and chaste.

With each step, enchantment leads,
Nurturing the ancient seeds.
A symphony of nature's song,
In every note, we all belong.

Across the night, the shadows dance,
Inviting souls to take a chance.
In the glow of fabled beams,
We find our hopes, our elven dreams.

So wander where the wild things weave,
In the magic, dare to believe.
For every path the heart may roam,
Leads back to love, to light, to home.

Glimmers of the Otherworldly Path

Through shadows deep, where whispers weave,
A light doth flicker, a tale to believe.
The moonlit glen, a secret art,
Calls forth the magic that stirs the heart.

Footsteps dance on ancient stone,
With every breath, the night is grown.
A tapestry of dreams unfolds,
In glimmers bright, the story told.

Voices murmur in twilight air,
As fae and sprites weave spells with care.
Each flick of wand, a spark alight,
Illuminates the dark of night.

Beneath the stars, where wonders play,
The otherworld awaits the stray.
Embark, dear soul, and take your chance,
In radiant glow, you'll find romance.

So heed the call of the silver path,
Hold tight to hope amidst the wrath.
For glimmers twine in every breath,
An echoing song of life and death.

Legends Inscribed in Luminous Leaves

In woods where sunlight gently creeps,
Legends rest in twilight keeps.
Each leaf a story, a truth profound,
With tales of magic all around.

The breeze carries whispers, soft as silk,
Of ancient heroes and dreams that milk.
In every rustle, a voice takes flight,
Guiding the wanderers through the night.

Rivers murmur of battles fierce,
As the universe weaves the threads it pierce.
Each drop a memory, a moment seized,
In luminous leaves, hearts are eased.

The nymphs dance under canopies wide,
With laughter and grace, they shall abide.
Their glow paints magic on the ground,
Where dreams and legends twirl around.

So seek the woods and dare to learn,
For in each leaf, a flame will burn.
The stories whisper your name so clear,
In luminous leaves, the truth draws near.

Echoes of the Sylvan Spirits

In sylvan depths where shadows blend,
The spirits weave, the echoes send.
Their laughter lilts on breezes fair,
A symphony of whispered air.

Between the trees, where secrets lie,
The ancient souls will teach you why.
In every glance, a spark ignites,
As woodland guardians share their sights.

From craggy roots to starlit skies,
The forest breathes, with watchful eyes.
Echoes ripple, from heart to heart,
In nature's choir, we play our part.

The queen of leaves, with crown of gold,
Threads stories of olden days bold.
While brothers of branches sway and bend,
Together in unity, they transcend.

As twilight drapes its velvet cloak,
The sylvan spirits gently spoke.
In echoes clear, their wisdom flows,
A dance of life, where magic grows.

Twilight's Breath on Elven Paths

At twilight's edge, where shadows kiss,
Elven paths weave dreams of bliss.
The air, it hums with magic bright,
Calling forth the stars of night.

With silver feet on mossy ground,
They stride through whispers, soft and sound.
Each step a pulse, each breath a tale,
Of love, of loss, where hearts prevail.

Moonbeams dapple the winding way,
Painting portraits at the end of day.
In every glimmer, secrets ensue,
In emerald shades, adventures brew.

The twilight winds, they weave and sway,
Guiding souls who seek to play.
In elven laughter, bright and clear,
The echoes of time seep ever near.

So wander forth, beneath the stars,
In twilight's breath, you'll find your scars.
Yet healing dwells in the night's embrace,
On elven paths, you'll find your place.

Murmurs Beneath Ancient Boughs

In hushed glades where shadows play,
The whispers of the past hold sway.
Ancient roots twist, stories unfurl,
Beneath the boughs, a magic swirl.

The breeze, it carries secrets old,
Of lovers lost and heroes bold.
Each rustling leaf, a tale to share,
Of moments caught in stillness there.

Moonlight dances on forest floors,
Painting dreams at twilight's doors.
Murmurs echo, soft and clear,
Inviting hearts to linger near.

In every crack and crevice found,
The wisdom of the earth is bound.
A world alive with every breath,
In nature's arms, a gentle death.

So tread with care on paths so wise,
For ancient dreams still softly rise.
Beneath the boughs, a vision gleams,
In murmurs spun from silver dreams.

Gossamer Dreams in Dusken Woods

In dusken woods where shadows lean,
Gossamer threads weave softly, sheen.
A tapestry of moonlit flight,
Where dreams take form in tender night.

Flickers dance in twilight's grace,
Whispering secrets in open space.
The air is thick with soft delight,
As gossamer dreams take off in flight.

Each step unveils a hidden lore,
Of ethereal beings, legends bore.
The branches weave a mystic sphere,
In every sigh, a heartbeat near.

Silence cradles the sleeping land,
Wrapped in twilight's gentle hand.
The veil between the worlds is thin,
Where soulful journeys deep begin.

So lose yourself in twilight's hue,
And find the magic waiting for you.
In dusken woods where wonders gleam,
Embrace the light of gossamer dream.

Phantoms of the Verdant Realm

In fields where emerald grasses sway,
Phantoms dance at the close of day.
They glide beneath the canopied sky,
Whispering tales as shadows fly.

Amidst the ferns and wildflowers bright,
Echoes of laughter, pure delight.
With each soft rustle, secrets unfold,
As the verdant realm preserves the old.

Windswept paths tell stories untold,
Of journeys taken, voices bold.
Through tangled vines, the phantoms weave,
A tapestry born of dreams we conceive.

So wander long in nature's grace,
And meet the phantoms, face to face.
In every whisper, a story's spun,
In the verdant realm where time is fun.

They guide the hearts that wish to roam,
In the embrace of the wild, our home.
With gentle whispers, they invite you near,
Phantoms dancing, forever here.

Veils of Starlit Secrets

Beneath a canvas of starlit dreams,
Veils of secrets float on moonbeam streams.
Each twinkling light holds a story near,
Of wishes made and lost in fear.

The night draws close, enveloping all,
In silken whispers, the shadows call.
A world transformed in silver glow,
Where hidden truths are free to flow.

The cosmic dance of dusk and dawn,
Echoes softly, a tender yawn.
With every heartbeat, a secret's kept,
In the silence where starlit shadows wept.

As night unfolds its vast embrace,
Ghostly figures in an endless chase.
Within these veils, the mystic thrives,
A realm where the essence of wonder thrives.

So gaze upon the celestial tide,
Where starlit secrets and dreams collide.
The universe hums its ancient song,
In veils of night, we all belong.

The Magic of Fading Echoes

In hidden glens where whispers dwell,
The trees remember tales to tell.
With every breeze, a story flows,
A dance of shadows, soft and slow.

In twilight's arms, the echoes gleam,
Like fleeting thoughts from a distant dream.
They waltz through time, both light and dark,
A symphony woven with a spark.

The lanterns flicker, secrets gleam,
In fading light, we dare to dream.
The magic lingers, magic stays,
In every heart, in quiet ways.

So gather near, refrain from doubt,
In fading echoes, we'll find out.
The stories told in whispered sighs,
Shall lift our hearts and help us rise.

For in this realm of soft retreat,
The fading echoes can't be beat.
They cradle hope, they set us free,
In every note, eternity.

Quiet Resilience in Shattered Silence

In corners dim where moments freeze,
Resilience whispers through the trees.
Though silence shrouds the world's refrain,
Hope blooms anew, despite the pain.

Each fractured hush, a chance to mend,
In shattered silence, hearts can blend.
With every breath, we find our way,
To weave the light into the gray.

The shadows cast may haunt the night,
Yet through the dark, we find our light.
A quiet strength begins to grow,
In whispers soft, we come to know.

Together, we shall tread the night,
With quiet courage, hearts alight.
For in the still, a spark ignites,
A chorus sung in silent flights.

So hold on close to dreams untold,
In every silence, let us be bold.
For strength is found in voices meek,
From quiet places, hope will speak.

Where Wonders Roam in Twilight

In forests deep, where shadows blend,
The twilight hour begins to send,
A tapestry of night and day,
Where wonders roam and spirits play.

With every step, the magic weaves,
A gentle song the twilight leaves.
The stars awake, in silence hum,
As dreams emerge, enchanting some.

Through whispering winds and murmuring streams,
The heart finds solace in moonlit dreams.
A world of wonder sits astride,
Where secrets bloom and fears subside.

So let us wander, hand in hand,
In twilight's glow, make our stand.
For here, where dreams begin to rise,
The wonders wait beneath the skies.

With eyes wide open, let us seek,
The magic that makes our spirits speak.
In twilight's hush, we find our place,
In endless realms of mystery and grace.

Songs of the Unseen Specters

In shadows cast by soft moonlight,
The unseen specters take their flight.
With gentle songs, they fill the air,
A haunting melody, rich and rare.

They dance through dreams, both near and far,
Guided gently by the evening star.
With whispers low, and voices sweet,
In spectral realms, our hearts shall meet.

They weave their tales of love and woe,
In every note, their truths bestow.
With every sigh, the past unfolds,
In songs of old, their magic molds.

So listen close, and you may find,
The songs of specters, sweet and kind.
In every echo, a chance to feel,
A bond with those, forever real.

For in this night, we shall not part,
The unseen specters touch the heart.
Together we shall sing their song,
In every note, where we belong.

Where Luminous Spirits Reside

In twilight's haze, they softly glow,
With whispers sweet from long ago.
A dance of light, they twirl and weave,
In secret realms, where none believe.

Through ancient oaks, their laughter rings,
A melody of forgotten things.
With every step on moonlit ground,
The wisdom of the ages found.

They guard the dreams that softly flow,
From hearts anew, to worlds below.
In potion'd air, their scents arise,
A glimpse of magic in their eyes.

Beneath the stars, they bid goodbye,
As dawn breaks clear in morning sky.
Yet in our hearts, their spark remains,
A gentle echo, love's refrains.

So listen close, when night departs,
For luminous whispers touch our hearts.
In every shadow, every sigh,
The spirits dwell, they never die.

Tattered Scrolls of Elysian Night

In dusty tomes, the tales reside,
Of moonlit paths where dreams abide.
With ancient quills and ink of stars,
They tell of magic, worlds afar.

Each parchment worn, with secrets bound,
A treasure trove of knowledge found.
Through whispered words, the past unfolds,
Of heroes brave and gallant souls.

In twilight's grasp, visions ignite,
A tapestry of dark and light.
With every page, a tale anew,
Of love and loss, of skies so blue.

They speak of creatures, wild and free,
Of realms obscured, of destiny.
In quiet corners, shadows creep,
Where ancient watching spirits weep.

So wander deep, let stories call,
In tattered scrolls, there's magic for all.
Unlock the doors, set history free,
Embrace the night, and let it be.

Dreamweavers in the Misty Thicket

In thickets deep, where shadows play,
The dreamweavers spin night and day.
With threads of silver, soft indeed,
They craft the visions that hearts need.

Through whispered winds, their secrets glide,
With starlit paths as their guide.
In every curl of foggy breath,
They dance with tales of life and death.

While moonbeams kiss the forest floor,
They weave the dreams of evermore.
With gentle hands, they shape the night,
A realm where hope ignites its light.

Each twilight hour, as shadows bloom,
They stir the stardust, weave the gloom.
From nestled hopes, to fears unknown,
In misty thickets, dreams are sown.

So seek the light in whispered haze,
Let dreamweavers guide your gaze.
Embrace the magic, let it flow,
In the thickets where dreams grow.

Cinders of Yore Beneath the Stars

Among the embers, whispers sigh,
Of ancient tales and lullabies.
In smoky veils of evening air,
The cinders speak, if one would dare.

Beneath the stars, their stories wake,
Of heroes bold and choices make.
With every flicker, shadows dance,
Awakening a long-lost chance.

From ashes cold, a warmth returns,
As firelight flickers, passion burns.
In quiet moments, hearts ignite,
A tapestry of dark and light.

So gather 'round, let voices soar,
In cinders of yore, forevermore.
A spark of memory, forever bright,
In the embrace of starry night.

Let fires burn, let shadows play,
For even in darkness, dreams find their way.
In every ember, hope persists,
The cinders whisper, and love exists.

The Hidden Symphony of Ghostly Breezes

In the glade where silence sings,
Whispers dance on velvet wings.
Moonlight weaves a silver thread,
Tales of secrets softly spread.

Branches sway, a gentle tune,
Echoes hum beneath the moon.
Notes unseen in dusky skies,
Channeling the lost goodbyes.

Each sigh carries an ancient spell,
An unseen world, a wishing well.
Through the mist, the voices call,
A symphony that binds us all.

Rustling leaves in twilight's grasp,
In their fold, all shadows clasp.
Embers of the past ignite,
With every rustle, every flight.

In this realm where spirits play,
Time stands still, the night holds sway.
An orchestra of sighs and dreams,
In the dark, the magic gleams.

Spirit's Embrace in a Dull Grasp

Within the room where memories fade,
Echoing footsteps, softly laid.
The air is thick with tales untold,
A gentle warmth against the cold.

Shadows linger, haunting light,
In the stillness of the night.
Fingers brush the faded seams,
Of longing hearts and distant dreams.

In every sigh, a story breathes,
With every turn, the heart believes.
Lurking ghosts in muted grace,
A spirit's dance, a soft embrace.

Bound in moments, lost in time,
Life and love in endless rhyme.
In the grasp of dusk and dawn,
The spirit waits, forever drawn.

Silent echoes fill the air,
A tender waltz, a whispered prayer.
In the stillness, find the spark,
Where love lingers in the dark.

Ethereal Tears on Twilight's Edge

On twilight's edge, the shadows weep,
Beneath the stars, the secrets creep.
A delicate dance of soft despair,
As night enfolds the whispered air.

Each tear glimmers like a star,
A tale of wishes, near and far.
Glistening drops on leaves of green,
Mirroring a world unseen.

Windswept tales of love and loss,
In each droplet, a cross.
Of laughter born from silent dreams,
And hope that lingers in moonbeams.

Gathering shadows in fading light,
Ethereal visions take their flight.
Tales of long-forgotten souls,
In the hush, the heart consoles.

Through the mist, an echo calls,
In the twilight, a soft enthralls.
Tears of time in beauty's guise,
A tapestry of silent cries.

Lost Whispers in Verdant Shadows

In the forest where secrets lie,
Lost whispers catch the wandering sigh.
Among the ferns and ancient trees,
The past unfolds upon the breeze.

Mossy carpets, a hushed embrace,
Every footfall finds its place.
Echoes linger in shaded glades,
Fleeting memories that time invades.

Ghostly figures weave through night,
In a dance of sheer delight.
Rustling leaves sing stories bold,
Of heroes past and tales retold.

Vines entwine like lovers' hands,
In this realm where magic stands.
Every rustle, every glance,
Captures time in a spectral dance.

Lost whispers haunt the twilight's breath,
Life and death in gentle quest.
In verdant shadows, truths emerge,
In every sigh, the spirits surge.

Secrets Beneath the Ancient Boughs

In the heart of the wood, shadows abound,
Whispers of secrets that dance all around.
Leaves softly rustle, a song in the night,
Tales of the ancients, hidden from sight.

Roots intertwine in a timeless embrace,
Guardians of stories, a sacred place.
Beneath tangled branches, the mysteries grow,
Of love and of loss, the trees seem to know.

Moonlight doth filter through canopies wide,
Illuminating paths where the lost spirits guide.
Fables of old weave through dreams in the dark,
Flickering lanterns left by a spark.

Time sways like branches, bending yet free,
In the arms of the forest, enchantment we see.
Echoes of laughter and sighs fill the air,
Weaving the tales of those who once were there.

So wander ye deeply, let wonder unfold,
In the heart of the wood, let your spirit be bold.
For every old whisper, a journey begun,
In the secrets beneath where the shadows do run.

Lost Laments of the Woodland Spirits

In the hush of the grove, where the shadows creep,
Spirits linger softly, in silence they weep.
Their voices a melody, lost in the wind,
Echoes of heartache from battles long sinned.

Their laughter like chimes through the glades of the past,
Remembrance of joy that was never to last.
Each sigh a reminder of love once held tight,
Now scattered like leaves in the chill of the night.

By the brook's gentle murmur, the stories unfold,
Of wishes ungranted and dreams left untold.
A tapestry woven with threads of despair,
In the twilight's embrace, their sorrows laid bare.

Yet amidst the lament, a glimmer of grace,
For the woodland spirits find solace in space.
With every lost tear that falls to the ground,
A new hope arises, in nature profound.

So heed the soft whispers that sway in the breeze,
For the spirits remind us, to seek and to seize.
In the heart of the forest, where shadows entwine,
The lost laments linger, a thread to divine.

Threads of Light in the Shaded Hollow

In the shaded hollow where sunbeams play,
Threads of light weave through, chasing shadows away.
A tapestry golden, a treasure unseen,
Filling the forest with magic serene.

Gentle the breeze, like a whispering friend,
Carrying secrets that nature can lend.
Moss-covered stones, bask in warmth's glow,
Guardians of secrets the wise will bestow.

The dance of the fireflies, erratic yet bright,
Flickers of hope in the cloak of the night.
Each glimmer a promise, a wish set afloat,
In the tranquil embrace of the forest's soft coat.

Nature's own canvas, alive with delight,
Each petal and fern bathed in soft, gentle light.
From dusk until dawn, mysteries pursue,
In threads of illumination, dreams glimmer anew.

So linger a while in this haven so fair,
Where the light finds a way through the branches of care.
Let your heart be a compass, your spirit take flight,
In the shaded hollow, find peace in the light.

Phrases Carried by Dandelion Wishes

On soft summer breezes, the wishes take flight,
Dandelion seeds drift, a beautiful sight.
Each whisper a promise, each puff a delight,
Carrying dreams that ignite the starlight.

As the sun dips below, painting skies in gold,
Children's laughter echoes, lives yet untold.
With each gentle breeze, seeds swirl and they dance,
Hopes gather momentum in a serendipitous trance.

A wish cast upon the air, yearning to land,
In fields of wildflowers, so vivid and grand.
Nature retrieves them, making magic anew,
For every dream whispered, a chance to renew.

Like the stories of old woven time after time,
Dandelions spark joy, in rhythm and rhyme.
Carried by whispers of dreams untamed,
They drift through the twilight, forever unclaimed.

So blow with intent, let your wishes arise,
With each puff of hope, send a piece to the skies.
The world holds its breath, and the magic will swish,
In the flight of the seeds, we find our true wish.

Whispers of the Muted Dawn

In the hush of morning light,
Dreams linger on the breeze,
Gentle whispers take their flight,
Waking hearts from slumber's freeze.

Softly glows the world anew,
Colors burst like wildflowers,
Nature sings in drops of dew,
Heralding the quiet hours.

Shadows dance with fading night,
Cloaked in mist, they blend and weave,
Echoes of a secret rite,
Tales of magic we believe.

With each breath, the dawn unfolds,
Stories held in sunlit streams,
Timeless wonders to behold,
Carried softly in our dreams.

As the sun begins to rise,
Hope awakens, bright and clear,
In the choir of the skies,
Dawn's sweet symphony we hear.

Fragments on the Sylvan Breeze

Beneath the canopy of green,
Whispers dance among the trees,
Magic lingers, softly seen,
Carried forth on gentle seas.

Leaves like laughter shiver soft,
Each rustle sings of age-old tales,
Where the hidden spirits loft,
In a world where wonder sails.

Twilight beckons with its glow,
Draws the night in velvet veil,
As the forest's secrets flow,
In the air, enchanting wail.

Hushed is every fleeting foot,
Nature weaves its sacred lore,
In the soil, the dreams take root,
Life returns forevermore.

Fragments of a sylvan hymn,
Softly play upon the wind,
In the heart, the light grows dim,
Yet the magic never ends.

Twilight Echoes in the Forbidden Grove

In the grove where shadows creep,
Secrets hide in twilight's grasp,
Voices call from depths of sleep,
Magic held in a silken clasp.

Every branch a story tells,
Glimmers caught in evening's sigh,
Where the ancient wisdom dwells,
Underneath the starlit sky.

Flickering lights like fireflies,
Guide the lost through tangled night,
As the silence softly ties,
Threads of wonder, pure delight.

Footsteps hush on mossy ground,
Every echo holds a spell,
In this space, the heart is found,
Among the whispers, magic swells.

Twilight dances with the breeze,
In the grove where few can roam,
Here, the night brings ancient keys,
Unlocking every heart as home.

Glimmers of the Fallen Faerie

In the glade where faeries tread,
Glimmers sparkle on the ground,
Whispers of the lives they've led,
Softly drifting all around.

Petals brush beneath their flight,
Every sigh a fleeting song,
In the depth of fading light,
Magic weaves a tale so strong.

Once they danced on evening's dew,
Now they linger, lost in time,
Echoes of a world anew,
Captured in a silver rhyme.

Fallen stars they left behind,
Shimmering in twilight's glow,
Every wish will surely bind,
Hearts that dare to seek and know.

Among the roots and muzzled dreams,
Glimmers beckon, soft and sweet,
In their light, our spirit beams,
Finding joy where faeries meet.

Echoes of Enchanted Sorrows

In twilight's embrace where shadows dance,
Whispers of woe weave a haunting trance.
Beneath the silvered moon's soft light,
Echoes of sorrows take their flight.

With lanterns dim, they sway and curl,
A tapestry spun of lost dreams' swirl.
Fragments of laughter, touching the night,
Lost in the depths of sorrow's might.

In gardens where petals fade and fall,
The secrets of hearts beneath the thrall.
Yet hope drips dew on the mourning ground,
A fragile heartbeat, a whispered sound.

With each soft sigh, the dark winds blow,
Carrying tales of joy and woe.
Yet through the mist, a glimmer glows,
A promise of light where beauty flows.

Let not the shadows claim your heart,
For in the dark, new dreams may start.
Embrace the night with courage bold,
For echoes weave stories yet untold.

Shattered Dreams in the Sylvan Mist

In the forest deep, where silence reigns,
Shattered dreams linger like soft refrains.
Veils of mist cloak the ancient trees,
Whispering tales on the gentle breeze.

Beneath the boughs of emerald green,
A world forgotten, a hidden screen.
Lost hopes shimmer in the pale air,
Dancing like fireflies caught in despair.

With each step tread, on moss so deep,
A thousand secrets this woodland keeps.
Ghosts of the past in a solemn glow,
Echo the wishes of long ago.

The twilight hums with a wistful sigh,
As echoes of laughter begin to die.
Yet in the gloom, a spark reveals,
The magic of dreams that fate conceals.

So wander forth, through mist and shade,
For broken dreams may yet cascade.
In sylvan depths, new paths will bend,
And shattered hopes can rise again.

The Veil Between Worlds

Between here and there, a thin veil lies,
Where whispers of magic dance in disguise.
A flicker of light on the edge of night,
Where dreams entwine in a waltz of flight.

With every heartbeat, the worlds align,
A shimmering border, a sacred sign.
What once was lost may gently return,
As shadows flicker and lanterns burn.

In the quiet hush of the twilight gleam,
Reality bends like a distant dream.
Past and present in a delicate swirl,
A tapestry stitched with fate's soft pearl.

At the crossroads of time, the ancients wait,
Guardians of fate, the weavers of fate.
With each choice made, a thread is spun,
A journey embarked, a race begun.

So dare to step through the glimmering veil,
Where light intertwines with a haunting tale.
For in the shifting, the heart may find,
The hidden truths this world has confined.

Resplendent Ghosts of Elden Wood

In Elden Wood, where the willows weep,
Resplendent ghosts in the shadows creep.
Their whispers float on the twilight air,
A symphony of secrets, woven with care.

With every rustle, a story unfolds,
Of ancient wisdom in echoes of old.
Flickering lights through the branches weave,
Weaving enchantments that none can perceive.

Around the glen, soft laughter rings,
Of bygone days and forgotten things.
Yet in their dance, there lies a truth,
The vibrant pulse of fading youth.

Caught in the twilight, they beckon near,
With promises sweet that time won't sear.
In their embrace, a comfort found,
A promise that dreams know no bound.

So wander softly 'neath the starlit skies,
For in Elden Wood, where magic lies,
The resplendent ghosts will guide your way,
Through the forest deep, where night meets day.

www.ingramcontent.com/pod-product-compliance
Ingram Content Group UK Ltd.
Pitfield, Milton Keynes, MK11 3LW, UK
UKHW021435290125
4349UKWH00039B/481

9 781805 644316